LIMA
(Peru)
The Delaplaine
Long Weekend Guide

TABLE OF CONTENTS

Chapter 1
WHY LIMA?

There are many things that you will find confusing in not only Lima, but the whole country of Peru as well, starting with its twisted and convoluted history, its fascinating if sometimes unappreciated ethnic mix of its population, all the way down to its mad drivers who create one of the worst traffic nightmares in any country I've visited. When you cross the street, do it with 3 or 4 others at the same time—maybe the crazy motorists will veer away from you.

There are thousands of taxis and busses filling the streets, and you will find some of the most dangerous traffic in the world right here in Lima. The buses come in many sizes: large ones, medium ones, small ones. Some of them are so packed you wonder how the occupants breathe.

Situated as it is on the Pacific coast, Lima rests on a massive cliff that rises 10 or 12 stories above the beach. It is quite dramatic.

There are hundreds of people hauling around backpacks and they all seem to be going to Cuzco and Machu Picchu. While I have always wanted to make the trek up into the mountains to see Machu Picchu, by the time I first got to Peru, Lima held far more fascination for me, so I skipped it.

You will quickly learn that the Incas, though they were dominant at the time the Spanish arrived to crush the natives under their Christian heels, were only the last in a long line of ancient cultures to inhabit the area.

If you're American or European (or from just about anywhere else), you will note that you are taller than the locals.

Many of the Indians have come out of the hills seeking work in Lima, which accounts for the high poverty rate around the city. You can spot them with their wide flat faces and prominent noses. Not a very attractive group, as a rule. The Peruvians I know personally are of European or mixed descent, and have white skins, reflecting their Spanish, Italian or German backgrounds. They consider themselves FAR above Indians as a class. (But I've noticed this in all South and Central American countries, this class snobbery.) In other countries (like Brazil) you will see people of different colors socializing, but not here in Lima.

One can find excellent restaurants with a variety of seafood and Chinese chifas. Archaeological ruins from pre-Hispanic Lima (1200 AD), gold museums with treasures from the Pre-Colombian and Inca periods, the church and catacombs of the convent of Francisco de Asises.

Nighttime cemetery tour. Presbitero Maestro is the cemetery where the remains of several important political military and literary figures are buried. It was the first municipal cemetery in Latin America founded between 1805 and 1808 and contains one of the largest collections of 19th century European marble sculpture in Latin America. The church and catacombs at San Francisco convent. The absolute highlight of the tour is a descent into the conference catacombs that served until 1808 as a burial ground. Quite extraordinary is that the monks arrange the remains according to bone types.

The Magical Water Circuit is located in the Parque de la Reserva. It is a wonderful collection of 13 ornamental and interactive fountains where the water music lights images and laser effects are combined in perfect union and harmony.

Gold museums. There are two gold museums, the Museo Larco with the largest collection of erotic archaeological art. The second, Museo Oro del Peru contains a wide assortment of pre-Colombian gold handicraft, weapons and ceremonial objects.

Pachacamac. Is an archaeological site 40 km southeast of Lima in the Valley of the Lurin River. It was dedicated to the most important God of the Peruvian coast in pre-Hispanic times, the Ichma Culture (1200 AD) and the Incas (around 1450 A.D).

Chapter 2
GETTING ABOUT

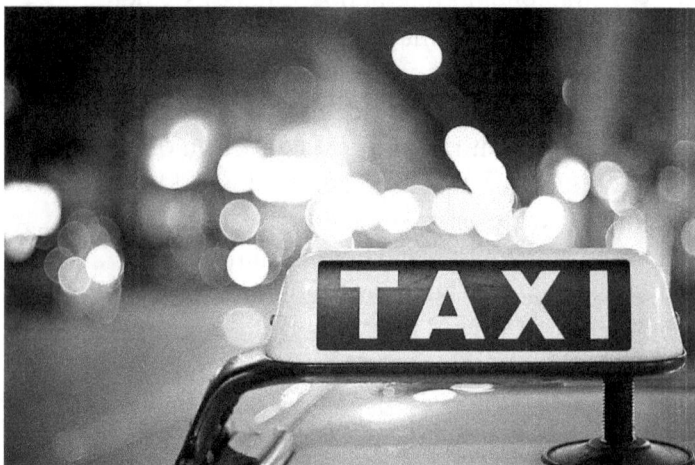

Because taxis do not by custom have meters, it's smart to have your hotel arrange airport pick-ups. They are used to doing this. If not, you can pick up a taxi at the airport.

Do not get into any taxi without first leaning through the window to negotiate the fare. If you get in first, you'll get screwed. If calling from your hotel, negotiate the price on the phone or have the clerks do it.

Most drivers will be consistent with the prices. Fares will run between 10 and 15 "soles," as the local currency is called.

Try to avoid the bus system unless you're already familiar with it. It's a nightmare.

Do not get into a taxi if someone else is already in it. Don't share taxis.

Be extremely aware of pickpockets.

Chapter 3
WHERE TO STAY

PRICELINE and **HOTWIRE**
www.priceline.com
www.hotwire.com
With Priceline, you bid on rooms in the part of the city where you want to stay, select whatever star levels you want, and generally can get cheaper rooms. These are usually in hotel chains, so nothing with too much character. With Hotwire, they tell you the price of the room. You don't bid on it. You can often play one site off against the other to get an even cheaper deal. (You don't find out the name of the lodging until you close the deal.)

3B BARRANCO'S
Jr. Centenario 130, Barranco, 51 1 247-6915
www.3bhostal.com
This B&B is for the budget-minded who don't mind simple yet modern lodgings. It's also good for those interested in nightlife, because it's not far from the area's busiest nightlife attractions. Even though it's

near the nightlife, it's still on a quiet street in the Barranco neighborhood. Rooms have cable TV. In the lobby where they serve breakfast, there's also a computer you can use. The place is decorated with art created by locals, a nice touch.

ARTS BOUTIQUE HOTEL B
Saenz Peña 204, Barranco 15063, Lima, +51 1 2060800
www.hotelb.pe
NEIGHBORHOOD: Barranco
This upscale hotel, set in a Belle Époque style mansion, offers elegant guest rooms. This hotel caters to people looking for an authentic historic atmosphere. It's connected to the Lucia de la Puente gallery. Amenities: Complimentary Wi-Fi and breakfast, plasma TVs with satellite channels, and iPod docks. Hotel facilities: formal restaurant, a bar, lounge with terrace seating, spa, and fitness room. Conveniently located near Kennedy Park, Huaca Pucllana and Gran Teatro Nacional.

B ARTS BOUTIQUE HOTEL
B HOTEL
HOTEL B

Sáenz Peña 204, Barranco, 51 1 206 0800
hotelb.pe.

NEIGHBORHOOD: Barranco

This hotel occupies a 1914 vintage mansion, now restored and gleaming white—whiter than the White house—and former seaside presidential summer residence that has been remodeled to house 10 guest rooms and an adjoining annex with another seven rooms. The two-year restoration involved rehabilitating marble floors and wood columns, while adding modern features like spacious bathrooms and Wi-Fi to rooms and a plunge pool and sun deck on the roof. Inside the whitewashed residence, recessed skylights brighten interiors and highlight a collection of contemporary art that adds a dose of modernity. The local celebrity chef Oscar Velarde of **La Gloria** restaurant designed the seafood menu in the dining room, one of several places on the property to eat out. The hotel is by a contemporary art gallery and I found the concierges to be most helpful.

BUSINESS TOWER HOTEL
Av. Guardia Civil, 727, Corpac, 51 1 319-5300
www.bth.pe
In the San Isidro financial district you'll find this hot
and trendy property frequented by business types
(hence the name). Sleek interiors are featured here
with loft-like rooms, all the amenities needed by
business travelers, and there's also a great restaurant
on premise. Near the **National Museum**, **Olivar
Park**, and **Huaca Pucllana**. Also nearby are **Lima
Golf Club** and **Kennedy Park**.

COUNTRY CLUB LIMA HOTEL
Los Eucaliptos 590, San Isidro, 611-9000
www.hotelcountry.com
Priceless paintings from the Museo Pedro de Osma
hang in the lobby and in each room in this luxurious
landmark. The colonial-style hotel, dating from 1926,
is itself a work of art, surrounded by even more
impressive embassies and homes of the elite. Just
follow the red carpet up the steps into the lobby,
where hand-painted tiles reflect the yellows and
greens of the stained-glass ceiling. The air of
refinement continues in the spacious rooms, with their
high ceilings, marble-topped desks, and beds draped
with fine fabrics and piled with pillows. Some have
private balconies that overlook the small, oval-shaped
pool or the grounds of the adjacent **Club Real**. Locals
come for high tea (Tuesday to Friday from 5 to 8) in
the stained-glass atrium bar, traditional Peruvian fare
in the elegant **Perroquet** restaurant, or a pisco sour in
the adjacent pub.

ESPAÑA
Jr. Azángaro 105, Centro Lima, 428-5546
www.hotelespanaperu.com
Near the Convento de San Francisco and just 4 blocks
from the Plaza de Armas, this extremely popular
budget hostal has a funky flair and communal
atmosphere
It occupies a rambling colonial building chock-full of
paintings, ceramics, faux Roman busts, plants, and
even the occasional mummy and skull. A maze of
rooms, most with shared bathrooms.

GRAN HOTEL BOLIVAR
Plaza San Martin, Jr. de la Union 958, Centro Lima,
619-1717
www.granhotelbolivar.com.pe

tastes may have changed since 1924, but this grand dame retains the grandeur of the days when guests included Ernest Hemingway. As you enter the marble-columned rotunda, your eyes are drawn upward to the magnificent stained-glass dome. Off to one side is the wood-paneled bar, which remains as popular as ever. The tables on the terrace are the perfect place to enjoy a pisco sour or a meal. The rooms are spacious, but some are a bit dog-eared. The hotel lacks some comforts and services, but the location is optimal, and the rates are quite reasonable. (If you pay a little extra, you can get a suite in front for an unforgettable view of Plaza San Martin.)

GRAN HOTEL BOLIVAR
Plaza San Martin, Jr. de la Union 958, Centro Lima, 761 9869
www.granhotelbolivar.com.pe

WEBSITE DOWN AT PRESSTIME
In a salmon-colored mansion (a pretty scary color when you first pull up to it) dating back nearly a century, this elegantly appointed hotel (formerly a private home) offers spacious, comfortable rooms and friendly service at a reasonable price. Black-and-white marble floors and crystal chandeliers greet you as you stroll through the antiques-filled lobby. You'll feel like you're in an embassy foyer. Up the wooden staircase are guest rooms with hand-carved furniture. Most rooms are in a newer annex in back, overlooking a courtyard garden with a graceful fountain. Known for its friendly service, the hotel sees repeat business year after year. A large restaurant in back serves breakfasts and traditional Peruvian fare.

HOTEL SAN ANTONIO ABAD
Av Ramon Ribeyro, 301, Miraflores, 447 6766
http://www.hotelsanantonioabad.com
Named for a saint, this clean and very friendly neighborhood hotel aims high. Its goal is to be welcoming and comfortable, and it succeeds. The colonial building, near the commercial center of Miraflores and several parks, has a garden terrace, fireplace, and sitting room.

BELMOND MIRAFLORES PARK HOTEL

Av Malecon de la Reserva 1035, Miraflores, 610-4000

www.miraflorespark.com

The elegant Miraflores Park Hotel bathes business executives and upscale tourists in unsurpassed luxury. It hugs the malecón, the park-lined avenue that follows the Lima coastline. I pick it for family friends and special clients and they don't complain. The rooms overlook Domodossola Park, the lobby-restaurant-bar is alive with guests.

From the moment you step into the elegant lobby with its polished marble floors and high columns, it is clear that this is one of the city's best hotels. The ocean-view rooms are gorgeous, and if you think the view from your room is breathtaking, just head up to the rooftop pool overlooking the entire coastline. City-view rooms, on the other hand, overlook an uninspiring residential neighborhood, so pay the extra money for an ocean view. Conservatively furnished guest rooms have sitting areas that make them seem like suites, sumptuous beds covered in luxe linens, and large marble bathrooms with separate tub and shower. The **Mesa 18** restaurant serves excellent nouveau Peruvian cuisine, whereas the **Dr. Jekyll and Mr. Hyde Bar** resembles an English pub.

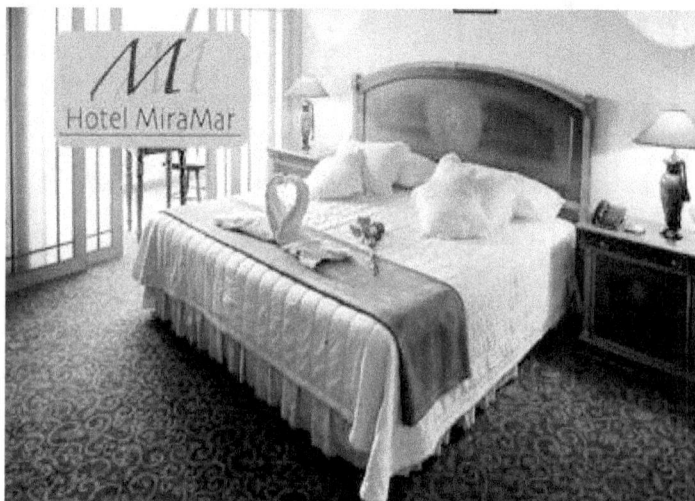

MIRAMAR HOTEL LIMA
Jr Bolognesi, 191, Miraflores, 51 1 2089700
www.hotelmiramarperu.com
"MiraMar Hotel" is located in the heart of Miraflores district, near to the most important financial centers, stores, restaurants, pubs, parks and the well known **Larcomar Shopping Center.** The rooms here are quite spacious, very functional furnishings with little or no charm.

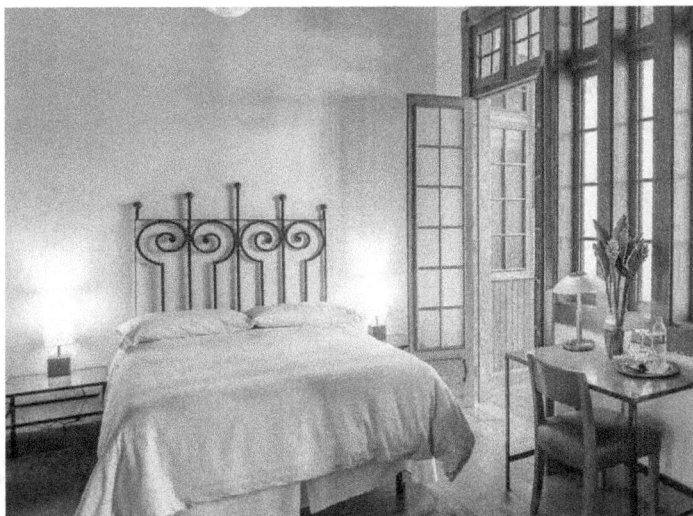

SECOND HOME PERU
Domeyer, 366, Barranco, 247-5522
www.secondhomeperu.com

This unique, small inn that hugs the coast was once the home of the well-known Peruvian painter and sculptor Victor Delfín. The idiosyncratic 1913 home is replete with artistic flavor -- and multiple works by Delfín. This 100-year-old Tudor-style house on a cliff overlooking the sea is one of Lima's loveliest lodging options. The home and gallery are a feast for the eyes, packed with art, surrounded by gardens filled with massive sculptures, and backed by a sweeping ocean view. Guest rooms on the second floor are tastefully simple, with hardwood floors, high ceilings, and lots of white; rooms 2 and 3 have ocean views. Three new oceanfront rooms built into the cliff have jaw-dropping views of the coast, though traffic noise from the road below could be a problem for light sleepers.

The owner, Lilian Delfin, can help with travel arrangements and other needs.

SHERATON LIMA HOTEL
Paseo de la Republica, 170, El Centro, 315-5000
www.sheratonlima.com
This massive hotel is a helpful landmark, as its concrete facade is visible from far away. Perfectly serviceable rooms have subdued colors, nice bathrooms, and giant windows with urban views. There are two buffet restaurants in the lobby; the Brazilian-style **La Cupula** serves grilled meats at your table, whereas the less expensive **Las Palmeras** has a folklore show on Friday nights. Popular with business travelers and tour groups alike, the hotel has a convention center, a small gym, and a pool that's open from December to May. Tourists appreciate its proximity to the city's historic district, but it is also near the expressway, so it's a quick drive to San Isidro, Miraflores, or Barranco. It's also relatively convenient to the airport.

Chapter 4
WHERE TO EAT

ACHE
H RESTAURANT
Av. La Paz 1055, Miraflores, 221-9315
CUISINE: Japanese
DRINKS: Full Bar
SERVING: Monday –Saturday lunch and dinner,
Sunday lunch
PRICE RANGE: $$$
No website
Hajime Kasuga's sleek Nikkei-fusion hot spot is
called Ache (the letter "H" sounds like "ache"
phonetically in Spanish).   Chef Kasuga is a third
generation Japanese-Peruvian. H has just about
everything: a restaurant with impeccable aesthetics
that serves fresh, refined and creative food
interpretations with subtle and clean flavors. It's

located just beside two other fusion restaurants --
Acurio's Italian-Peruvian restaurant, **Los Bachiche**,
and Pedro Miguel Schiaffino's Amazonian restaurant,
Amaz. There are the basics, sushi and sashimi, and
then *tiradito*, for which he wraps the fish around
shredded turnip, adding an entirely new texture to
each bite without altering the flavor. He has the
Cebiche Roll, his personal take on the *Maki
Acevichado* that uses a *leche de tigre* based sauce on
top of the roll rather than a mayo one, as well as duck
and prawn meatballs, scallops lit on fire in their shells
as they are served, and sirloin that sits on a bed of
Peruvian cacao.

AMAZ
Av. La Paz 1079, Miraflores, 221-9393
www.amaz.com.pe
CUISINE: Amazon

DRINKS: Full bar
SERVING: Mon – Sat lunch and dinner, Sunday lunch only
PRICE RANGE: $$$
Amazonian bar and restaurant in Miraflores. 120-seat tropical chic Amaz sources all wild and organic products. The restaurant brings many obscure Amazonian ingredients to Lima, where few even realize they exist. Dishes bounce around from updated traditional Amazonian dishes such as *pataraschca*, where fish is cooked inside of a banana leaf, to oversized Amazonian snails drizzled with a sweet chorizo dressing. A hot sauce flavors *aji* peppers from the Amazon with star anis. The cocktail menu, a definite high point, combines pisco with underutilized fruits such as *taperibá* and *cocona* in more than a dozen original cocktails.

ANTICA PIZZERIA
Av. Primavera 275, San Borja, 51 1 3721336
www.anticapizzeria.com.pe
CUISINE: Italian
DRINKS: Full bar
SERVING: Daily noon - midnight
PRICE RANGE: $$
Warm, rustic, wood fired pizza (over 50 kinds) in this cozy ambience with rough-hewn tables surrounded by old pots and pans hanging from the walls; the rafters hold wooden barrels. Casual and good.

ANTICUCHOS DE LA TIA GRIMANESA
466 Ca. Ignacio Merino, Miraflores, 514 421 468
CUISINE: Peruvian
DRINKS: No bar
SERVING: Mon – Sat dinner, Sunday closed
PRICE RANGE: $$
The most venerated *anticuchos* (heart of cow) in all
of Lima are grilled at this corner cart, which has been
tended to by the legendary Doña Grimanesa for more
than 30 years. The meat is so tender and the house-
made hot sauces so delicious, that it's no wonder the
wait is often more than an hour. The best bet: show
up at 6:45pm and wait for Doña Grimanesa to roll up
or telephone your order in ahead of time.

ASTRID Y GASTON
Av. Paz Soldan 290, San Isidro, 442-2777
www.astridygaston.com
CUISINE: Peruvian, International
DRINKS: Full Bar
SERVING: Mon-Sat lunch and dinner, closed Sun
PRICE RANGE: $$$$
This is a chic modern colonial dining room and cozy
bar where Gastón Acurio has been one of Peru's
celebrity chefs for many years, with a burgeoning
empire of fine-dining restaurants not only in Lima but
also a handful of other cities in both North and South
America (including San Francisco) and a cooking
show on TV.

BAO?
Calle José Domingo Choquehuanca 411, +51 977 499 865
https://www.facebook.com/baoacomer/
CUISINE: Japanese/Asian Fusion/Vegan
DRINKS: Beer & Wine
SERVING: Lunch, Dinner
PRICE RANGE: $$
NEIGHBORHOOD: Miraflores
Quite a Spartan atmosphere. Very basic. You order and then grab a table where you can eat. This small eatery serves a wide variety of Bao sandwiches and Rice bowls. Pulled pork & shitake; Short ribs & seaweed. Take-out available.
Vegetarian/Vegan/Gluten-free options.

BRUJAS DE CACHICHE
Calle Bolognesi 472, Miraflores, 447-1133
www.brujasdecachiche.com.pe
WEBSITE DOWN AT PRESSTIME
CUISINE: Criollo
DRINKS: Full Bar
SERVING: Mon-Sat lunch and dinner, Sun noon-5pm

PRICE RANGE: $$$$
The "Witches of Cachiche" celebrates 2,000 years of local culture with a menu that's a tour of the "magical" cuisines of pre-Columbian Peru. The chef even uses ancient recipes and ingredients. Corvina sauce with grilled shrimp; lasagna stuffed chicken chili; shrimp tambal.

CENTRAL RESTAURANTE
Av. Pedro de Osma 301, +51 1 2428515
https://www.centralrestaurante.com.pe/
CUISINE: Peruvian
DRINKS: Beer & Wine
SERVING: Lunch, Dinner
PRICE RANGE: $$$$
NEIGHBORHOOD: Barranco
Flagship restaurant of Chef Virgilio Martínez Véliz. Elegant eatery is considered one of the top restaurants in the world. A "closed door" restaurant that you have to book in advance. (Months in advance, I might add.) The bleached rough-hewn brick stone walls provide a nice contrast to the white tablecloth service. Sophisticated tasting menu offers seasonal dishes. Unique dishes featuring local seafood and meats. It will be beyond your expectations. A large glass partition divides you from the kitchen, and you can watch the 10 or so people back there cooking away. Wine pairing. The door is not marked, so don't walk by this place.

CHEZ WONG

Calle Enrique Leon Garcia, 114, Santa Catalina, 470-6217

No website

CUISINE: Asian -Peruvian

DRINKS:

SERVING: Lunch only, noon to 3 weekdays if the chef feels like it

PRICE RANGE: $$$$

Javier Wong's home kitchen, cebicheria, has been much praised as the place to get the best ceviche in all of Lima. That's just a crock of shit. There are dozens of places where you can get very fine ceviche. It's basically the national dish of Peru. And why this old man who cooks in what is basically the garage next door to his house gets credit for preparing the absolute best would have to do with Anthony Bourdain, who said as much on his TV show. It will also be the most expensive ceviche you will have in Lima. (Even the bottled water is a ripoff.) You must speak Spanish even to get a reservation. Wong comes out and cooks in front of the customers. He filets the fish (it is almost always flounder), makes the ceviche, and then you will get a hot plate that will be some sort of Chinese dish. Same menu basically every day. Ceviche, tiradito, Chinese. Not a nice part of town. Be carful negotiating with taxis.

CLUB LAMBAYEQUE RESTAURANT
Av. Del Ejercito 977, Lima, +51 – 2218656
https://www.facebook.com/comedorclublambayeque/
CUISINE: Peruvian / Chiclayo
DRINKS: Beer & Wine
SERVING: Lunch
PRICE RANGE: $$
NEIGHBORHOOD: Miraflores
Peruvian cuisine serving spicy ceviche and tortillas in a bright room with floor-to-ceiling windows. Everybody knows that Peruvians make the best ceviche in the world, but those who know even more say that the best ceviche in Peru comes from the northern part of the country, and this is the food served here, specifically, from Chiclayo. Get the torrejitas de choclo, tortilla de raya, and cabrito con frejoles. Impressive selection of Peruvian beers. Usually has some live music.

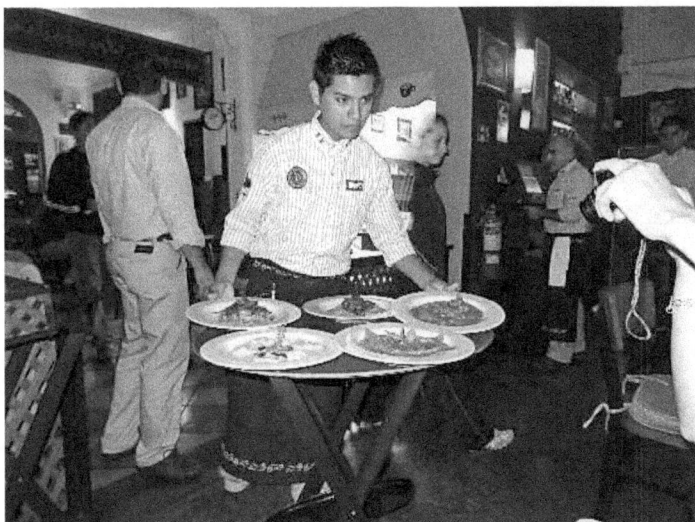

DANICA
Av. Emilio Cavenecia, 170, San Isidro, 421-1891
www.danica.pe
WEBSITE DOWN AT PRESSTIME
CUISINE: Italian, Mediterranean, Peruvian
DRINKS: Full Bar
SERVING: Mon-Sat 12:30pm-12:30 am; Sun 12:30-10:30pm
PRICE RANGE: $$

The interior is casual, looking more like an upscale café than a fine-dining destination, and though you can get Italian comfort food, Vanessa Siragusa also turns out some very creative and elaborate fusion dishes. If there's one dish (besides the scrumptious desserts) to highlight, it might be the stir-fried beef risotto, a cross between Peru's mainstay lomo saltado and risotto (though the raviolis de asado, or roast meat ravioli with mustard sauce, comes in a close second).

EL MERCADO
Av Hipólito Unanue 203, Lima, +51 974779517
www.rafaelosterling.pe
CUISINE: Peruvian
DRINKS: Full Bar
SERVING: Lunch only
PRICE RANGE: $$
NEIGHBORHOOD: Miraflores
Top chef and author Rafael Osterling offers a menu that pays homage to Peruvian cuisine, particularly ceviche. Menu features dishes like Grilled octopus and Fish Roe Sandwich. Beautiful courtyard and open kitchen.

EL RINCON QUE NO CONOCES
Calle Bernardo Alcedo N° 363, Lince, Centro, +51 923 520 174
www.elrinconquenoconoces.pe
CUISINE: Peruvian, Creole
DRINKS: Full Bar
SERVING: Tues-Sun noon-4:30pm
PRICE RANGE: $$
Although stuck in a bit of a no-man's land (at least for tourists) -- at the edge of the Centro -- this authentic, amiable, old-school Peruvian criollo restaurant, helmed by Teresa Izquierdo Gonzáles, a 70-something institution of a chef, is worth the trek. Doña Teresa has been cooking here for more than 30 years, and her neighborhood eatery may have gotten a little more polished and popular (it's even welcomed

Rachel Ray of Food Network through its doors), but it hasn't deviated from its mission: classic Creole cooking.

EL SENORIO DE SULCO
Malecon Cisneros 1470, Miraflores, 441 0183
www.senoriodesulco.com
CUISINE: Peruvian
DRINKS: Full Bar
SERVING: Monday-Saturday lunch and dinner, Sunday lunch
PRICE RANGE: $$$
The owner of this restaurant, Isabel Alvarez, has written several cookbooks. The antique cooking vessels hanging on the walls reflect her passion for traditional Peruvian cuisine. Start with one of various cebiches or *chupe de camarones* (a creamy river prawn soup) if in season, then move on to *arroz con pato* (rice and duck with a splash of dark beer), *congrio sudado* (a tender whitefish in a spicy broth),

or *huatia sulcana* (a traditional beef stew). Weekend lunch buffets offer an excellent opportunity to sample a variety of Peruvian cuisine.

FIESTA
Avenida Reducto, 1278, Miraflores, 242-9009
www.restaurantfiestagourmet.com
CUISINE: Northern Peruvian
DRINKS: Full Bar
SERVING: Daily 12:30-5pm and 8-11pm
PRICE RANGE: $$$
Latin themed South Beach style martini lounge. Cuisine Chiclayo. Pisco-flambeed shrimp and milk braised goat. The bar seats around 20 people. It is a nice comfortable environment where you can have a drink or wait for your party. They have a signature drink called El Capitán del norte made with macerado de mamey. On the second floor there's Ceviche and Champagne Bar, where you can have ceviche made on the spot and drink champagne. It seats about 90 people in very comfortable chairs. The decoration is sober with colorful orange chairs. Plenty of mirrors

give the impression of a larger room, and therefore you won't feel as if in a crowded, small place. This is not a restaurant to have a quick lunch. Most lunches usually last about 2-3 hours.

ISOLINA

Avenida San Martin Prolongacion 101 | Esquina Con Calle Domeyer, Lima, +51 2475075
http://isolina.pe/
CUISINE: Peruvian
DRINKS: Full Bar
SERVING: Lunch & Dinner
PRICE RANGE: $$
NEIGHBORHOOD: Barranco

José del Castillo, the restaurant's chef and owner, specializes in traditional home cooked dishes of Peru. Most of the food you get in restaurants mixes the Chinese and Japanese influences that now dominate Peruvian cuisine, but before that, there was "criollo," their version of Creole, which mixes Spanish and African slave influences. You usually get this type of food in the country or in people's homes. Here it's the specialty. Menu favorites include beef kidneys, chicken gizzards, pigs feet, tacu tacu (sautéed rice and bean patties), *osso buco estofado* (meat so tender because it's cooked for 4 hours in red wine you can eat it with a spoon). But you can also get superb sea bass ceviche with fried octopus. I always over order when I come here, but I can't help it. The food is so different and delicious. All dishes are large and serve several people. Traditional cocktails.

JUANITO DE BARRANCO

Avenida Almirante Miguel Grau 270, +51 941 536 016

https://www.facebook.com/eljuanitodebarranco/

CUISINE: Peruvian
DRINKS: Full Bar
SERVING: Lunch, Dinner
PRICE RANGE: $ / cash only
NEIGHBORHOOD: Barranco

Trendy (but nothing fancy, just the opposite) eatery filling a very narrow sliver of a space—the high ceilings make it appear to be much larger. Frequented by bohemians, writers and artists. Family owned and operated place. Very friendly people. Menu of traditional Peruvian cuisine – mostly sandwiches and ceviche. The sandwiches are really good, and cheap. Cash only.

LA 73 PARADERO GOURMET

Avenue El Sol 175, Lima, +51 1 2470780

www.restaurantela73.com

CUISINE: Peruvian/South American
DRINKS: Full Bar
SERVING: Lunch, Dinner, & Brunch
PRICE RANGE: $$
NEIGHBORHOOD: Barranco

Comfortable eatery set in an elegant old 19th Century house with indoor and outdoor seating. Menu features creative twist on classic Peruvian cuisine. Menu picks: Pulpo a la parrilla (Tangy marinated octopus tentacles) and La güera (spaghetti with aji amarillo cream and sautéed shrimp). The *lomo saltado* (fried steak served with potatoes) that you can get all over town is particularly excellent here. Great selection of desserts, like the decadent churros that are filled with dulce de leche.

LA CANTA RANA
Genova 101, Barranco, 247-7274
CUISINE: Ceviche, Seafood
DRINKS: Full Bar
SERVING: Tues-Sat 11am-11pm; Sun-Mon 11am-6pm
PRICE RANGE: $$
A relaxed and informal place (in local lingo, a huarique) that looks almost like the interior of a garage and is immensely popular with locals, "the Singing Frog" is the very definition of a neighborhood cevichería. The menu lists 15 types of sea bass, including one stuffed with langoustines, as well as lots of varieties of ceviche.

LA COSTA VERDE
Playa Barranquito, Barranco, 247-1244
www.restaurantecostaverde.com
CUISINE: Seafood
DRINKS: Full Bar
SERVING: Daily noon-midnight
PRICE RANGE: $$$$
Costa Verde, perched on a promontory jutting out into the ocean along the "green coast" south of Miraflores, is probably as expensive a meal as you'll have in Peru (unless you go to **Chef Wong's**). The big-time seafood buffet is what makes everyone's eyes bulge. There's a daily lunch buffet and also a huge gourmet dinner buffet, which the restaurant

claims is registered in the Guinness Book of Records. (It's not in my copy.)

LA PICANTERIA
Francisco Moreno 388-Surquillo | Esquina Con Cuadra 6 de Gonzales Prada, Lima, +51 2416676
www.picanteriasdelperu.com
CUISINE: Peruvian/Latin/Seafood
DRINKS: Full Bar
SERVING: Dinner; closed Sundays
PRICE RANGE: $$$
NEIGHBORHOOD: Surquillo
Located in a renovated one story, nondescript building, this popular eatery offers a rotating menu of Peruvian delicacies. Favorites: Catch of the day (served three ways) and Puplo (Octopus). They're famous for their homemade chicha de jora–a type of fermented corn drink. (People love it, but it turns my stomach.) I prefer their house-brewed beer. Reservations recommended.

L'EAU VIVE
Ucayali 370, Centro, 427-5612
CUISINE: French, Peruvian
DRINKS: Wine and Pisco
SERVING: Mon-Sat 12:30-3pm and 7:30-9:30pm
PRICE RANGE: $$
The restaurant, run by a French order of nuns, donates its proceeds to charity. In a colonial palace 2 blocks from the Plaza de Armas and across the street from one of Lima's most important mansions, Torre Tagle, it features several large dining rooms with high ceilings. It's one of the most unusual places I've ever

dined. The nuns sing "Ave Maria" promptly at
9:30pm.

LE CAFE
Swissotel Lima
Avenida Santo Toribio 173, +51 1 4214400
http://www.swissotellima.com.pe/
CUISINE: Peruvian
DRINKS: Beer & Wine
SERVING: Breakfast, Lunch, & Dinner
PRICE RANGE: $$
NEIGHBORHOOD: Miraflores
Café offering a menu of Peruvian and 'International'
dishes. Daily breakfast and lunch buffet – also has an
a la carte menu. Nothing terribly out of the ordinary,
as it's a hotel restaurant with nothing really to
distinguish it. A "safe" place to eat. Large selection of
pastries and desserts. Vegetarian/Vegan options.

NANKA
Jr. Bambues 198, +51 1 369 7297
Calle Manuel Banon 260, +51 1 467 8417
https://www.nanka.pe/
CUISINE: Peruvian
DRINKS: Full Bar
SERVING: Breakfast, Lunch, Dinner
PRICE RANGE: $$$$
NEIGHBORHOOD: Miraflores / San Isidro
Has 2 locations each offering creative spaces that are
cheerful and fun, the ultra-high ceilings allowing their
decorator to do some interesting fresh things with
wood and stone. Seasonal menu designed for sharing.
Favorites: Ayacucho Guinea pig and Artichoke

ravioli. Gluten-free/Vegetarian options. Creative cocktails. Outdoor dining in good weather. s

NUEVO MUNDO BAR MIRAFLORES
Calle Manuel Bonilla 103, Miraflores, +51 999 136 156
https://www.facebook.com/NuevoMundoBarLima/
CUISINE: Pub
DRINKS: Beer & Wine
SERVING: Lunch, Dinner
PRICE RANGE: $$
NEIGHBORHOOD: Miraflores
Popular pub known for its large selection of local beers. (The biggest selection in town on draft, I think.) Simple bar stools at high-top tables keep the attitude here very casual. Colorful wall murals will keep your eyes busy because you can't take your eyes off them. Bar grub like hamburgers, alitas, a good chicken burger and tequenos. Live music.

MAIDO
Calle San Martin 399, Lima, +51 1 313-5100
www.maido.pe
CUISINE: Japanese/Sushi
DRINKS: Full Bar
SERVING: Lunch & Dinner
PRICE RANGE: $$$$
NEIGHBORHOOD: Miraflores
Creative menu of sushi made in a Peruvian kitchen. Menu picks: Wagyu beef and Peruvian inspired ceviche. Excellent cocktails. Reservations a must.

LIMA
PERUVIAN
GOURMET

MALABAR RESTAURANT

MALABAR
Calle Camino Real 101, San Isidro, 440-5300
www.malabar.com.pe
CUISINE: Peruvian; Amazonian
DRINKS: Full Bar
SERVING: 12:30-4pm & 7:30-11pm Mon-Sat
PRICE RANGE: $$$
Pedro Miguel Schiaffino uses obscure Amazonian
ingredients like alpaca prosciutto and cocona berries.
With all of the attention paid to Peruvian food in
recent years, the cuisine of the Amazon has been all
but ignored. Schiaffino is changing that. At his Lima
restaurant Malabar he uses ingredients from the
Peruvian Amazon, the country's largest and least
populated region, and he has spent a decade
developing a relationship with producers there. This
place should be on your top 5 spots to consider when
visiting Lima.

MARAS
Calle Amador Merino Reyna 339, San Isidro, +51 1
2015023
Calle las Begonias, 450

www.marasrestaurante.com.pe/
CUISINE: Latin/Peruvian
DRINKS: Full Bar
SERVING: Lunch/Dinner/Late night
PRICE RANGE: $$$$
NEIGHBORHOOD: San Isidro
Attached to the Westin Hotel, this restaurant offers an innovative menu featuring dishes like Causa, Tiraditos and fresh fish. Favorites: Suckling pig. Vegetarian and Gluten-free options. Amazing selection of wine. Nice destination for Peruvian cocktails.

MAYTA
Av. Mariscal La Mar 1285, +51 1 4226708
www.jaimepesaque.com
CUISINE: Peruvian
DRINKS: Full Bar
SERVING: Sunday – Friday lunch and dinner, Saturday dinner

PRICE RANGE: $$$

This chilled out restaurant bar is ground zero for pisco geekery in Lima. Mayta is a great example of what makes eating in Peru so delicious and interesting. The restaurant décor is modern yet has a warm feeling. The bar area is separate from the dining area and has a long bank of windows looking out on to the busy corner. Their specialty cocktail is the *chilcano*. This is a refreshing blend of pisco, ginger ale, lime juice and sugar syrup. With 35 different choices of pisco flavors you will never get tired of ordering the Chilcano. Over 100 clear glass bottles are set up behind Mayta's bar, like an apothecary's shop, filled with piscos vibrantly infused with local ingredients like camu camu, yucca, ginger, rose petals and litchi, eucalyptus, mandarin and coca leaves, used to flavor variations of the Chilcano. The tall, refreshing drink, purportedly introduced by 19th-century Italian immigrants, combines pisco with ginger ale, bitters and a splash of lime juice. You can try a flight of 5 small Chilcanos before going to the dining room for a delicious, nine-course tasting menu (tuna ceviche, guinea pig confit, etc.).

OSSO

Tahiti 175, Lima, +51 1 3529915
www.osso.pe
CUISINE: Steakhouse/Butcher Shop
DRINKS: Beer & Wine Only
SERVING: Lunch & Dinner; Lunch only on Sun
PRICE RANGE: $$
NEIGHBORHOOD: La Molina

Renzo Garibaldi, one of the best butchers in the world, runs this rustic steakhouse. This is a meat-lovers dream. Menu features aged Peruvian, Angus and Wagyu steaks. Try the toffee dessert made with beef cheeks. Nice selection of Peruvian craft beers. Note: only seats 10.

PESCADOS CAPITALES
Avenida La Mar, 1337, Miraflores, 421-8808
www.pescadoscapitales.com
CUISINE: Ceviche, Seafood
DRINKS: Full Bar
SERVING: Daily lunch and dinner
PRICE RANGE: $$$
With an easygoing, hip style that's similar to Cebichería La Mar's, this upscale ceviche and seafood restaurant is popular with Lima's gente bella (beautiful people). The name is a sly riff on the phrase for "original sin" (pescado, or fish, being just

one letter removed from pecado, or sin); the dishes have names like "ire," "envy," and "avarice," and the menu declares that a few larger dishes are for the "vain or gluttonous." The restaurant has a large open-air terrace where overflow crowds sip pisco sours and beers on weekend afternoons, and a big, airy, and busy dining room under a high bamboo and glass roof.

RAFAEL
San Martin, 300, Miraflores, 242-4149
www.rafaelosterling.com
CUISINE: Asian – Mediterranean – Peruvian
DRINKS: Full Bar
SERVING: Monday – Friday lunch and dinner, Saturday dinner, Sunday closed
PRICE RANGE: $$$
The 15-table restaurant is housed in a vivid red mansion built around the turn of the last century. Inside there's a modern interior and Art Deco details,

very warm and welcoming. Don't let the traditional atmosphere here fool you—the Asian and Mediterranean-influenced Peruvian dishes, such as *lomo saltado* made with rice vinegar and pisco, are exquisitely prepared by the chef-owner Rafael Osterling Letts. Pizza, prosciutto, figs, basil and pine nuts is a good starter, or go with the ceviche of sole, scallops and black baby clams, and tiradito Nikkei – yellowfin tuna sashimi with yuzu (a Japanese citrus fruit), mirin (rice wine), guacamole and smoky sesame oil. Mains include a stew of North Peruvian grouper cheeks with vongole, calamari and confit potatoes, and a Peruvian dish of rice and puy lentils with pan-fried foie gras, river shrimp, scallops and roast banana. Quite a place, this.

RESTAURANT HUACA PUCLLANA

General Borgoño, cuadra 8, Miraflores, 445-4042
www.resthuacapucllana.com
CUISINE: Nouveau Peruvian
DRINKS: Full Bar
SERVING: Mon-Sat 12:30pm-midnight; Sun 12:30-4pm
PRICE RANGE: $$$$
With knockout views of the pyramid and secluded in the midst of Lima's chaotic jumble,
the low hump of adobe bricks and excavation walkways are illuminated at night, and diners can take a tour of the construction and digs after dinner. Fried shrimp with quinoa crust; broiled scallops with Parmesan cheese and lemon butter; Hot shrimp ceviche, marinated in lime and chilli sauce, served in a steaming stone bowl; Shrimp in coco-curry sauce with eggplant chunks and fried rice.

RESTAURANT SONIA

Agustin Lozano La Rosa 173 Chorrillos, Lima, +51-669 249-6850

http://www.restaurantsonia.com/

CUISINE: Peruvian/Seafood

DRINKS: Beer & Wine

SERVING: Breakfast, Lunch, Dinner

PRICE RANGE: $$

NEIGHBORHOOD: Miraflores

This is another of the "closed door" restaurants you find in Lima, so book ahead. It's just as popular with locals as it is with tourists, so there's a good mix of people here. Always lively. Outdoor seating under some colorful netting is a good choice if the weather's good. Inside, it's as quaint as it could possibly be, with the red brick walls, quotes painted onto the walls. Known for their Ceviche, this eatery also offers a menu of traditional Peruvian seafood dishes. The whole fried fish is delectable—crunchy and crispy skin on the outside and incredibly moist flesh inside. Live music. But you can order anything they have and you'll be pleased.

SEGUNDO MUELLE
Av. Los Conquistadores 489, San Isidro, 635-5555
www.segundomuelle.com
CUISINE: Ceviche; Seafood
DRINKS: Full Bar
SERVING: Daily 12-5
PRICE RANGE: $$
Famous for its shrimp dishes, but it also offers
exquisite seafood plates such as Chicharrón de
Mariscos (fish cracklings), Parihuela (spicy fish and
shellfish soup), Conchitas a la Parmesana (grilled
shellfish with grated cheese on top), Pulpo al Olivo
(octopus in black olive sauce), and many more
mouth-watering selections. Exotic drinks and beers.
The restaurant has two stories and wide open terraces.
It is situated in the financial district of San Isidro, is
open everyday and also offers a valet parking service.

WA LOK

Jr. Paruro, 878, Barrio Chino, Centro, 958-4722
Av Angamos West, 700, Miraflores, 447-1329
www.walok.com.pe
CUISINE: Chinese
DRINKS: Full Bar
SERVING: Daily lunch and dinner
PRICE RANGE: $

One of the best and well-known *Chifas* (local slang
for Chinese restaurants) is appropriately situated right
in the heart of the Barrio Chino, in the center of Lima.
(There's also a location in fashionable Miraflores.)
Hot or cold drinks accompany its colorful Oriental
dishes. The dining area is spacious and distinctly
Chinese. Tourists frequently flock here for the
combination Chinese-Peruvian cuisine, after trekking
about the nearby historic center of the city. A
delicious Dim Sum and a traditional noodle and
dumpling breakfast can be enjoyed when this Chifa
opens in the early hours of the morning.

Chapter 5
NIGHTLIFE

AURA
Av. Angamos 2681, +51 1 2681598
Open: Wednesday - Saturday 11:00pm – 5am
This high class, two level Miraflores disco is pricey, trend setting, and full of well-dressed, beautiful people. This is where Lima's upscale youth come to kick loose and meet other upscale youth. A good mix of foreign visitors make their way to the disco as well. The high-energy dance floor atmosphere is contrasted with the large outdoor patio that faces the Pacific. A number of VIP rooms are available for those that need it. Music tends to focus on American

and British pop, with some techno, Latin pop, and
rock thrown in.

AYAHUASCA RESTOBAR
Avenida Prolongacion San Martin 130 Barranco, 981-
044-745
www.ayahuascarestobar.com
Open: Monday - Saturday 8pm – 3am
Multi-room lounge, the tipple of choice is pisco,
which shows up in unexpected cocktails with camu
camu berry juice and coca leaves. Laid back evenings
morph into ultra-hip nights with a cool crowd
wandering in between midnight and 3am.

BIZARRO
Calle Francisco De Paula Camino 201, Miraflores,
446 3508
www.bizarrobar.com

Bizarro Bar is a bastion of culture in the '90s and continues to maintain a vibrant scene to this day. Come catch the live music with great cocktails.

LA NOCHE
Pasaje Sanchez Carrión 199 A Barranco, 247-1012
www.lanoche.com.pe
Underground local groups, popular national acts. The action rages from 11pm until wee hours fueled by cheap cervezas and pisco sours. An oversized upper level room offers rotating art exhibitions. They're closed on Sunday but on all other nights they have very decent gigs in one of their three bars. All kinds of music but mainly rock, jazz or trova. Many really good Peruvian artists play here on regular basis. In the main bar where no concerts are played you can have Spanish or Peruvian snacks and all kinds of drinks at normal local price. This well-known tri-level bar is *the* spot to see rock, punk and Latin music acts in Lima.

Chapter 6
WHAT TO SEE & DO

-CENTRO LIMA-

LA CATEDRAL DE LIMA
East side of Plaza de Armas, El Centro, 427-9647
www.arzobispadodelima.org
The first church on the site was completed in 1625.
The layout for this immense structure was dictated by
Francisco Pizarro (who's buried here), and his basic
vision has survived complete rebuilding after

earthquakes in 1746 and 1940. Inside are impressive baroque appointments, especially the intricately carved choir stalls. Because of changing tastes, the main altar was replaced around 1800 with one in a neoclassical style. At about the same time the towers that flank the entrance were added. Admission fee includes a 40-minute tour. Visit the chapel where Pizarro is entombed and the small museum of religious art and artifacts.

MONASTERIO DE SAN FRANCISCO
Jr. Ancash 471, El Centro, 426-7377
www.museocatacumbas.com
Bones—including thousands and thousands of human skulls—are piled in eerie geometric patterns in the crypt of this church. This was the city's first cemetery, and the underground tunnels contain the earthly remains of some 75,000 people, which you visit on a

tour (available in English). **The Church of Saint Francis** is the most visited in Lima, mostly because of these catacombs. But it's also the best example of what is known as the "Lima Baroque" style of architecture. The handsome carved portal would later influence those on other churches, including the **Iglesia de la Merced**. The central nave is known for its beautiful ceilings painted in a style called *mudejar* (a blend of Moorish and Spanish designs). On the tour you'll see the adjoining monastery's immense collection of antique texts, some dating back to the 17th century.

MUSEO DE ARTE DE LIMA
Paseo Colon 125, El Centro, 204-0000
www.mali.pe
Built in 1871 as the **Palacio de la Expedicion**, this mammoth neoclassical structure was designed by the Italian architect Antonio Leonardo, with metal columns from the workshop of Gustav Eiffel (who later built the famous Parisian tower). The ground floor holds temporary exhibitions, usually by international artists, whereas the second floor houses a permanent exhibition that contains a bit of everything, from pre-Columbian artifacts to colonial-era furniture. One of the highlights is the collection of 2,000-year-old weavings from Paracas. Leave time to sip an espresso in the café near the entrance.

MUSEO DEL CONGRESO Y DE LA INQUISICION
Jr. Junin 548, El Centro, 311-7777 Ext. 5160
www.congreso.gob.pe/museo/index.html

Visit the torture chambers of the Spanish Inquisition, where life-size exhibits illustrate methods of extracting "confessions" from prisoners accused of crimes against the Catholic Church. You can only visit the museum on hourly tours, and they offer just a few tours in English per day, so you'll want to reserve ahead of time. In contrast to the grisly displays, the 18th-century building is quite lovely, especially the coffered ceilings.

PARQUE DE LA RESERVA
Av. Petit Thouars, Esquina con el Jiron Madre de Dios, El Centro, 424-0827
www.parquedelareserva.com.pe
The Lima municipal government has transformed a dusty park on the edge of the downtown area into a delightful tour of dancing water and lights — more than a dozen fountains send water shooting into the air, choreographed to music and light. **The Magic Water Circuit (*Circuito Mágico del Agua*)** is the

city's newest attraction, and locals and tourists agree it's surprisingly awesome. Check it out for yourself. The fountains are open Wednesday through Sunday, from 4 p.m. to 10 p.m., but go after the sun has set to see the light show; modest admission.

PLAZA DE ARMA
Jr. Junin and Jr. Carabaya, El Centro, 980-048-502
No website
This massive square has been the center of the city since 1535. Over the years it has served many functions, from an open-air theater for melodramas to an impromptu ring for bullfights. Huge fires once burned in the center for people sentenced to death by the Spanish Inquisition. Much has changed over the years, but one thing remaining is the bronze fountain unveiled in 1651. It was here that Jose de San Martin declared the country's independence from Spain in 1821.

-BARRANCO-

ARTESANOS DON BOSCO
Av San Martin 135, Distrito de Lima, 713-1344
www.artesanosdonbosco.org/es/
An Italian missionary in the 1970s founded the Don
Bosco cooperative and began promoting the
handiwork of woodworkers from provincial Peru. His
efforts continue at this studio and showroom in a
restored century old building where visitors can
watch Andean villagers transform wood blocks into
masterful chairs, benches, and cabinets.

BAJADO DE LOS BANOS
1 blk. west of Parque Municipal
http://www.munibarranco.gob.pe

A brick promenade lined by pastel houses, ficus tress and bright bougainvillea leads from the plaza to a spectacular ocean overlook crossed by the Puente de los Suspiros, a slim wooden walkway where lovers linger. The cobbled road that leads down to the "Baths"—the beaches—is shaded by massive trees and lined with historic architecture. Once the route that local fishermen used to reach their boats, it is now a popular promenade at night, since many of the former homes that line it hold restaurants and bars. At the bottom of the hill a covered wooden bridge spans a busy road, called **Cirquito de Playas**, to a coastal sidewalk that leads to several beaches and restaurants. A short walk to the north is Playa Barranquito, and Playa Agua Dulce is half a mile south.

GALERIA DEDALO
Paseo Saenz Pena 295, Barranco, 652-5400
No website
One of the coolest art galleries. A great, relaxed little place which sells furniture, traditional and contemporary crafts and some food. Beautifully displayed items, including some Bonzai plants, and orchid cuttings, which may (or may not) be brought back to the States. Check with Customs. The back of the shop is an open courtyard where coffees, pizza, and light snacks are served. Great cappuccino. The shop is only one block from the cliffs overlooking the Pacific.

MUSEO PEDRO DE OSMA
Av Pedro de Osma 42`, Barranco, 467-0063
www.museopedrodeosma.org
This ivory-hued mansion houses the private collection
of Pedro de Osma Gildemeister, an aristocrat who
hosted dignitaries and helped put Barranco on Lima's
society map. His collection of colonial-era Peruvian
paintings, textiles, sculptures and books offers a
glimpse into the traditional culture that shaped the
neighborhood over a century ago.

PARQUE MUNICIPAL
Bordered by Av. Miguel Grau and Av. Pedro de
Osma
No website
Chess players, couples and tourists rendezvous in this
central green space that is at times tranquil and other
times buoyant, with open-air salsa classes, a
revolving cast of buskers and free weekend concerts
by regional rock and pop stars in the amphitheater.

The Parque Municipal in the center of Barranco is a nice place to sit down, relax or just to see and to be seen. The park was opened in 1899. In the center of the park stands a Venus statue, known as 'La Donaide,' surrounded by a fountain. Here you find as well the "Biblioteca Municipal de Barranco", built at the end of the 19th Century. The unique tower was added in 1911. Formerly, it housed the local government; today it houses the public library. Just opposite is the "Iglesia de la Santisima Cruz." Every evening around 6pm local artists show and sell their work. The park is very popular at night as it is surrounded by many clubs and bars.

PUENTE DE LOS SUSPIROS
One block from Parque Municipal, Barranco
No website
The Bridge of Sighs (*Puente de los Suspiros*) is a lovely wooden structure spanning the Bajada de Baños, a stone walkway that runs down to the Pacific through Lima's bohemian district, Barranco. This comely neighborhood was the place to be in the 19th Century and retains its laid-back charm today; there are lots of bars and restaurants in Barranco, plus views of the water, and it's worth strolling around here for an afternoon.

-SAN ISIDRO-

PARQUE EL OLIVAR
Av. Los Incas between Choquehuanca and Arce, San Isidro, 513-9000
www.msi.gob.pe
The olive grove here dates back 5 centuries. For years this rambling olive grove was slowly disappearing as homes for wealthy citizens were being built on its perimeter. The process was halted in the 1960s, in time to save more than 1,500 gnarled olive trees. Some of the trees are more than a century old and still bear fruit. A network of sidewalks, flowerbeds, fountains and playgrounds make this 50-acre park a popular spot on weekend afternoons.

HUACA HUALLAMARCA
C Nicolas de Rivera 201, San Isidro, 222-4124

Adobe pyramid. The sight of this mud-brick pyramid catches many people off guard. The structure, painstakingly restored on the front side, seems out of place among the neighborhood's towering hotels and apartment buildings. The upper platform affords some nice views of San Isidro. There's a small museum with displays of objects found at the site, including several mummies. This temple, thought to be a place of worship, predates the Incas.

-MIRAFLORES-

PARQUE KENNEDY
Av. Mariscal Oscar Benavides, Miraflores
www.atlasobscura.com/places/parque-kennedy
Parque Central and Parque Kennedy unite to form one large park in the heart of Miraflores. At daytime it's a beautiful place to have a little break and enjoy yourself. Here you find the Municipality of Miraflores, the main church "Virgen Milagrosa," a small information point (unfortunately they mostly only speak Spanish), a playground for the little ones and some nice restaurants and street cafés. Vendors sell yummy typical Peruvian sweets like "picarones" (a kind of donut prepared with yam or squash flour seasoned with cinnamon, anisette and salt and fried in oil). In the afternoons and on weekends craftsmen and artists sell their work and sometimes musicians

entertain everybody who wants to listen. Especially on weekends Parque Central and Parque Kennedy are the place for small fairs, crafts markets, family and cultural events. In the evenings the parks are a favorite meeting place for young people.

RICARDO PALMA HOUSE
Gral Suarez 189, Miraflores, 617-7279
https://antipode-peru.com/en-map-ricardo-palma-house
This house was the home of the Peruvian author Ricardo Palma from 1913 until his death in 1919.

HUACA PUCLLANA
Calle General Borgoño cuadra 8, Miraflores, 617-7148
www.huacapucllanamiraflores.pe
This 72-foot tall and over 300-foot wide adobe brick ceremonial mound is located in trendy Miraflores. Visitors can climb the platforms for spectacular views

and then tour a museum stocked with pottery and textiles found at the site.

MUSEO ARQUEOLOGICO AMANO
Ca Retiro, 160, Miraflores, 442-2909
www.museoamano.org
This is a very fine private collection of artifacts from the Chancay, Chimú and Nazca periods, once owned by Yoshitaro Amano. It boasts one of the most complete exhibits of Chancay textile examples and is particularly interesting for pottery and pre-Columbian textiles, all superbly displayed and lit.

PARQUE DEL AMOR
Malecón Cisneros, Miraflores
No website
In the Parque del Amor (Love Park), the design borrows heavily from Antoni Gaudí.
Keep walking a few minutes north of the Parque del Amor, and you'll see the taking-off point for parasailers. The Malecón is the prime spot for parasailing in Lima — gliders jump off the cliffs and ride the winds whipping off the ocean below. (Not for me, thanks.)

POLI MUSEUM
Lord Cochrane 466, Miraflores, 422-2437
No website
Enrico Poli has gathered one of the most impressive private collections of archeological objects of Inca and other pre-Columbian cultures as well as colonial art in Peru. Displayed are fantastic ceramics, gold and silver pieces, paintings and wooden sculptures. This

museum (basically his house) is really worth a visit. The collection gathers together so-called huacos (ceramic pieces), paintings, gold, silver and wooden sculptures. Mr. Poli will guide you through this place in person. Appointments should be made in advance.

OTHER THINGS

PACHACAMAC
Km 31 of Old Pan-American Highway
www.pachacamac.net
Pachacamac is located within the confines of metropolitan Lima, about one hour by taxi from San Isidro/Miraflores, at Kilometer 31 of the auxiliary road that runs along the southern Pan-American Highway. A tour of the site can take several hours. Located in the Lurin River Valley, 9 miles south of Lima, this sprawling complex was an important pilgrimage spot along Peru's central coast both in the time of the Incas and before. Most of the common buildings and temples were built c. 800-1450 CE, shortly before the arrival and conquest by the Inca Empire.

PARQUE LAS LEYENDAS
Av. Las Leyendas 580 - 582 – 586, San Miguel, 717-9878
https://leyendas.gob.pe/botanica/
There is much more to the "Park of Legends"—the zoo was built right inside Lima's most extensive ancient city. This is one of the most important pre-Hispanic complexes in the central Peruvian coast called the Archaeological Complex of Maranga and today it houses some museums, various Huacas (Adobe Pyramids) and the beautiful Botanical Garden. Located between Central Lima and Callao, this **zoo** covers Peru's major geographical divisions: coast, mountains and jungle. There are up to 210 native animals, with a few imports (such as hippos).

Chapter 7
SHOPPING & SERVICES

AGUA Y TIERRA
Ernesto Diez Canseco 298, Miraflores, 444-6980
No website
A tidy shop that specializes in crafts from the
Shipibo, Aguaruna and Asháninka cultures from the
Amazon.

ANTIGUEDADES SIGLO XVIII
Av. La Paz 397, Miraflores, 445-8915
No website
This silver shop specializes in ornate picture frames
and *milagros,* or miracles—heart-shape charms that

are placed at the feet of a saint's statue as the physical representation of prayers.

BOTERIA NEGREIROS
Calle Las Casas 041, San Isidro, 442-0599
Sturdy leather boots from a single master craftsman.

EL TUPO
Calle Los Libertadores 551, San Isidro, 440-0537
www.eltupo.com.pe
Fine handmade silverware created by people who know what they're doing. They do all their own designs as well as produce all the items they sell.

CAMUSSO
Av. Ricardo Rivera Navarrete 788, Lima, +51 981 519 088
www.camusso.com.pe
For sterling you can't beat the classic designs at Camusso, a local *plateria,* or silver shop, that opened its doors in 1933. Call ahead for a free guided tour of the factory, which is a few blocks west of El Centro. There's also a shop in San Isidro at Avenida Rivera Navarrete 788.

ILARIA
Av. Dos de Mayo 308, San Isidro, 512-3530
www.ilariainternational.com
WEBSITE DOWN AT PRESSTIME
Silverware, jewelry, and decorative items. The art
pieces are made using traditional and ancient
Peruvian designs. They have over 20 stores in Peru.

INDIGO
Av. El Bosque 260, San Isidro, 440-3099
www.galeriaindigo.com.pe
On a quiet street in San Isidro, Indigo lets you wander
through at least half a dozen different rooms filled
with unique items. There's a selection of whimsical
ceramics inspired by traditional designs, as well as
modern pieces. In the center of it all is an open-air
café.

JOCKEY PLAZA
Javier Prado Este 4200 Surco, 716-2000
http://www.jockeyplaza.com.pe
One of the leading shopping centers in Peru. Great to go shopping for the latest fashions. There are also cute areas to sit and have coffee and a sweet.

KUNA
AV. Larco 671, Miraflores, 447-1623
www.kuna.com.pe
Lots of stores stock clothing made of alpaca, but Kuna is one of the few to also offer articles made from vicuña. This cousin of the llama produces the world's finest wool. It's fashioned into scarves, sweaters, and even knee-length coats. Another location on Avenida Jorge Bassadre in San Isidro.

LA LÍNEA DEL TIEMPO
Av. La Paz 648, Miraflores, 303-2248
No website
A lot of excellent religious art can be found here.
They buy, sell and restore ancient art works as well as
contemporary items. A wide variety of works in
bronze, wood, pewter, porcelain, ceramics, silver.

LARCOMAR
Malecón de la Reserva 610, Lima, Peru, 6254343
http://www.larcomar.com/
This shopping center is right on the cliff, so you have
a fantastic view of the ocean. Here there are a few
shops, restaurants, a movie cinema, theatre, bowling,
and other special events.

LAS PALLAS
Jr. Cajamarca 212, Barranco, 477-4629

www.laspallas.com.pe
WEBSITE DOWN AT PRESSTIME
Run by an expat Scottish woman who has spent years scouring Peru for goods and cultivating relationships with local craftsmen. Las Pallas has folk art and crafts from all of Peru's diverse regions, with weavings, pottery, masks, hand painted frames and trays, baskets, charms, amulets. Also, carved gourds, retablos, appliques and much more.

MERCADO INDIO / INDIAN MARKET
Blocks 52 to 55 of Av. Petit Thouars, Miraflores
No website
A crafts-market strip stretching four blocks (Blocks 52 to 55) along Avenida Petit Thouars in Miraflores. Everything from bric-a-brac to fossilized shark teeth is available in literally hundreds of shops. Be wary of cheap deals on silver (likely low grade) or artifacts and fossils, which are legal to buy, but illegal to take out of the country.

POLVOS AZULES
Avenida Paseo de la Republica, Cuadra 4
www.polvosazules.pe
1,500 merchants sell pirated copies of anything and everything. Hundreds of stores offering clothes, shoes, sports gear including running shoes and trekking boots, backpacks, bags, toys and perfumes, a wide range of electronic equipment. You get among many other things TVs, MP3 and MP4 players, Playstations, Wii's, CD and DVD players, cell phones, all sorts of accessories and of course (mostly pirated) music CDs and movie DVDs.

INDEX

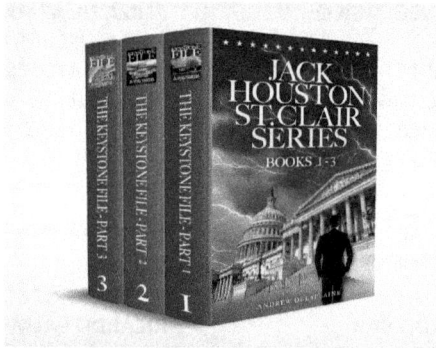

WANT 3 FREE THRILLERS?

Why, of course you do!

If you like these writers--
Vince Flynn, Brad Thor, Tom Clancy, James Patterson,
David Baldacci, John Grisham, Brad Meltzer, Daniel
Silva, Don DeLillo

If you like these TV series –
House of Cards, Scandal, West Wing, The Good Wife,
Madam Secretary, Designated Survivor

You'll love the **unputdownable** series about
Jack Houston St. Clair, with political intrigue, romance,
suspense.

Besides writing travel books, I've written political thrillers
for many years that have delighted hundreds of thousands
of readers. I want to introduce you to my work!
Send me an email and I'll send you a link where you can
download the first 3 books in my bestselling series,

absolutely FREE.

Mention **this book** when you email me.

<u>andrewdelaplaine@mac.com</u>

LIMA

The Delaplaine 2021 Long Weekend Guide

Andrew Delaplaine

GET 3 FREE NOVELS
Like political thrillers?
See next page to download 3 FREE page-turning novels—no strings attached.

NO BUSINESS HAS PAID A SINGLE PENNY OR GIVEN *ANYTHING* TO BE INCLUDED IN THIS BOOK.

Senior Writer –*James Cubby*
Senior Editors - *Renee & Sophie Delaplaine*

Gramercy Park Press
New York London Paris

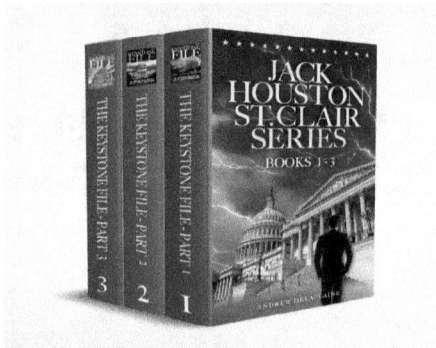

WANT 3 FREE THRILLERS?

Why, of course you do!
If you like these writers--
Vince Flynn, Brad Thor, Tom Clancy, James Patterson,
David Baldacci, John Grisham, Brad Meltzer, Daniel
Silva, Don DeLillo
If you like these TV series –
House of Cards, Scandal, West Wing, The Good Wife,
Madam Secretary, Designated Survivor

You'll love the **unputdownable** series about
Jack Houston St. Clair, with political intrigue, romance,
and loads of action and suspense.

Besides writing travel books, I've written political thrillers
for many years that have delighted hundreds of thousands
of readers. I want to introduce you to my work!
Send me an email and I'll send you a link where you can
download the first 3 books in my bestselling series,
absolutely FREE.
Mention **<u>this book</u>** when you email me.

andrewdelaplaine@mac.com